Published by Nauset Press

nausetpress.com

Wareham, MA

Cover and Book Design: Nauset Press
Cover Image: Public domain, *Chalice of Saint John the Evangelist* (1470–1475) by Hans Memling

ISBN: 978-1-962890-03-8
Library of Congress Control Number: 2023949109

Poems in this collection have appeared in: *First Literary Review-East* and in the chapbook *Sweetwater Ardour* (Yavanika Press) and the chapbook *Come, Ghost* (Triple Series, Ravenna Press).

ARBOR VITÆ

MAUREEN ALSOP

NAUSET PRESS

WAREHAM, MASSACHUSETTS

To Lilia

I held a posting in a small room

at the armoury.

Not a window.

Nor the sun's repetition across the terrain.

I held no permission to imagine,

but we'd spoken several times.

I was a supplicant on earth seeking

no claim, no cause

Interiors at the hill camp

    —grafted and sometimes spacious

we were lain   as into

    closets   cupboards

corner to corner or in hallways

with doors across

and air between

Love is not always beautiful

and not

this love on this hour on this earth

I think of you at first light.

The crude undertakings began as a blur

through the trees—a tug into darkness—

the bare view of flannel weed, coral bell,

and finger grass—an ambiguity the body refuses.

Let the water gently break thee.

There was a sodden forest half a mile beyond

the city from where you came—

where the grasses bent

into that patch of green

The twice travelled night closed

over the sleeping village

The dawn turned slowly

its zenith toward me

The horses were gone and a few cows, like a vow,

lingered in the open mud.

What you never meant to say fell

upon the open river

Sometimes you became someone you recognized

It was all night after I told you

Yesterday today

is over

You don't have to know emptiness to know

the body's wound

The sun fell the first day after the war

neither peace nor loneliness was buried

beneath the earth.

We would start from what rescue held in us—

I wanted to leave, to follow

the river, and return to the small house

I wanted to measure what

remained to measure us.

I didn't say your name with softness I didn't say

your name.

Through one door, your messages

flooded the room. Through the other

door, in periphery, you saw

willowy figures dart. They lived

as apparitions in the night's

various levels. They waited for love. They lived,

hallucinogenic: triangles and fractal neon patterns,

Agrippa red or pale tamarisk, scent of glasswort

and smoke-rings, they floated—moonlit up the wall.

Somewhere in all of this, a horizon exists, a farm

on the other side of the acacia, palmyra, millet.

I think about the means by which trauma enters

the body. It is like water

entering the body of a swimmer

until the water permeates the cells

and particle by particle

the swimmer and the ocean

hold one another.

I think about the unfolding

as a strange compassion

and how in our dislocation

we are estranged from ourselves.

In this moment of awakening,

intimacy is a bridge.

There is a time for this, love's evolution

lifts out of the soil, bodily, without denial, finds domain,

it is not a physical existence. It is a boat

at the edge of a black lake where

we gather to row through the night.

I found the watching place

under the tick of a wave.

You said it would hit me, the weapon

of the mind, a slowing

                of breath— small

small horses, gentle

                break thee.

The short edge of a mirror in one light.

Almost alone.

Almost forgotten.

Victory dies when the treaty is signed.

If you love a certain shadow, love mine.

Here sang the shot which straightened the floodplain.

The citizens here were not rebels.

Which battle did you choose?

Under which breeze did you surrender.

When I explain it to you, you will understand—

For you who asked, and you who continued—but I don't want

to tell the condition set forth when I accepted the request

From what sea did I trace you—

What town did I invent—

I will make it there

to these remains of you—

I measured

the men's weight in each scar of the sidewalk—

as if to be taken into constellations

at the water's edge—long signs

strange animal greetings

Is there a need yet to explain a split in our consciousness?

After the accident, at the beginning,

my eyes closed with each exhalation. I wanted

to choose what exists,

to imbue what is just.

I took clarity in my belief.

You asked about my country.

It was slow. I waited to move. My injury

was reviewed. It was quiet.

I turned my back.

Signs faded.

Restrictions grew. My country,

where I was, it didn't exist.

What was said, how to yield, what

was not said. I relished the taste of our language.

You lost your family in the raid. You never declared your
injury. In atonement, consciousness would be observed.

You'd always kept things hidden from others
These things you were trying to control

Your limits, visible now, the canyon's imperfection—
their bodies lay in the glen past the grinding stone.

As you lowered the dead into place—there was no other

cultivation, the bloodroot failed, salve upon

the tongue of each small life.

We die together within our words

the light going out

the evening a spell   or something sweeter—

with precision

the barn door closes to the wind

and the whaler horses fade

You found square lettering in the clearing where fingers
turned once pages.

As you remembered, you remembered my hand darkening,
the touch, the sound of graphite.

And you stood and watched as if leaning against a fourth door-
way.

You loved three words hidden in the text, you loved
the greenery and the groves which you might touch.

You did not lose the body's first sharpness.

I was met among the prophets, anonymous,

anointed, a seeker. I was assigned

between rivers.

I will not close my heart to language. The waters

which connect me to symbol. Phrase by phrase

to grandmothers and fathers so far past.

The heat of my body

　　　would be short lived. And I heard only

in the moment what my guide provided—a diagram,

a leaching of earth's interior.

I was taught to restructure each dream with completion.

Pausing, you heard carriages carried away, a series of trees'
thud under a locking axe.

You held a need to name the horses.

A warmth greased their body and glass walls
enclosed the pasture.

The pasture fills with smoke. You disappear
into a photograph of fire.

It was in my sleep you returned.

You saved me against artillery—spared the massacre.
I never reached the tower at the fort. We travelled
south where the snow splintered the river and deer
froze deep in mud.

The Baedeker guide ended at the arroyo Hondo

bees abandoned the currents and slow moths passed south

onyx veins along the ridgeline, razor wire, the dirt

wild in dry weathers marked

our time

Through the copper scented night, through traces

in the scent of blood, you come.

I can read you.

A life in the mind of the dead

reaches the living.

Like the serpent's milk, the zephyr, and the owl.

I never knew in advance

what would happen, though

I have come close on occasion.

To tie yourself to the dead, is to provide truth to the abasement.

A bank of reeds separates the past.

My hand falls asleep

    under my night pillow, where I clutch at the grass—

        a space where the seer's myth pressures the earth's crust.

Possessed by bereavements, as a number is assigned

    and tagged to my right breast.

You were one of the dead who would not wait. You didn't understand.

Your skin was sore when you walked through

the alders. The skin of a ghost disappearing in angles.

Silence alights trees

under the treeless silence.

Slow the body becomes whole

Everything came into view. The world asleep; not

even within it now the light

of the old traditions.

The earth above. Wordless.

We dropped formalities.

We dropped through atmospheric miles.

We touched the shape within

the light which excised each darkness.

I woke with the bell.

And I ended the bell.

I died under the ringing.

In an arid haunting over a thousand terrains, over

diagrams pinned in duress as locations. The map

marked a landscape where the lease was paid in advance.

Why would they resist. After a time,

closer and closer, the remote

desert crept nearer.

The wind in the mind

flowered into the sound of a bell.

We dreamed slow wounds.

I am an assassin to my own measures. I measured
the light. But when I think of it, when I think
of the light, it's fair to say that light assumes its place.

And it is fair enough to promise
an attraction to the earth exists. And the earth,
briefly gives, but in counterturn, folds
a devastation toward us.

Meanwhile, the earth exalts the spirit.
And in my mind, I must say, there
were pleasant effects, the light,
a yellow soot—ochre yarrow—
like the center of their lips.

In dreams you came to me the night after it happened.

When I say it happened, it was less than an accident.

I never knew what you accounted

from interrogations.

What darkness in the machine, your actor.

As if the disbelief of the body is heroism,

a bronze commendation laid

in the bronze grass.

A halo breaks the horizon wide.

An impersonal failure begins.

Some think it impossible to be hard, to be uneven.

Some think that *what happens to you will not happen to me* because

each experience is limitless.

Think again ghost, something sweeter, a gateway at the edge
of the aquifer.

I know where you live, my little ravening, a dark speck
in the imagination.

You left no short passage through my grief.

Yes, in the pre-dark of that century,

we spoke in reversals.

The immodest horizon held no desire.

Along the snowbanks   I was able

to follow the road drenched with stars   Soon

the sun was spinning

in two directions—

Outside, the young men came,

shameful now it seems, their advance.

The first fray of death hung

in German doorways.

There were physical needs the earth filled—

tender with horses

Order, the only ritual—

was evening bread, the one hour

of the night the small French candles burned

The men came back, but different.

Time, a helpless medicine—serrated edges of cottonwood leaves

Hunger—like rooms we stood in— a balm

purpled at the heart

On the trains home we expected their return from an

afterward—

apple   night   orchards   flowering

wind-swamped places

where blossoms roar into a bright taste

It was easy to return

the apology in seven dialects

A half-century passes.

Somewhere between what I want to do

and what I am

Sashay, witness

      My boots behoof

Come, you said

and the boundary shifted.

You were cautioned

but forgot

      the gift of speaking, a wilderness

           a language beyond you cannot go

Tonight the valley is a mirror you stand before.

You cross the snow, descend

into the medicine cabinet.

Tap water runs red, then to dust.

Each of your slow movements, slower than the last

The river backs into, then buckles the room

No longer a body to see or to touch

No longer this body to remember

I was sent to see a fullness in winter.

Winter, a dank corridor, a familiar lust, a fear.

Winter, a list of chores and hungers—

a crooked sky, a question—fire

        lifts over an open snow field.

The evening sun behind the hill seems tall.

Sun-burnished pines bury the telling.

You never knew my name

was lost, my body

I called after you

        but sometimes it was only a call for the sea—

  smoke fumes in the shape of cuttlefish

It was the sound of someone saying my name

but I couldn't hear them.

The sun going down

The sun not yet

risen—

to emerge slowly it is forward

and you would like to turn back

It is the salt-stained night—

marsh throat in the night

There is a scar-trail

       space   the horses stripped.

Halfway, eyes the distance, then leans, a horse,

running toward flames,

dusk horse & lantern.

All that goes   goes with it

         It is all that goes with that

A stone fence you follow—

the same north lake

The snow waits on us

It is a good deep snow

        And deep ash where

the beloved is not

forgotten

One where the war

is now

a softly glow

softly, a move of air

the glow is beautiful here

beautiful

and mad

——the glow of the world

this one hour love

lifts away

Maureen Alsop, Ph.D. is the author of *Tender to Empress; Pyre; Later, Knives & Trees; Mirror Inside Coffin; Mantic; Apparition Wren* (also a Spanish Edition, *Reyezuelo Aparición;* translated by Mario Domínguez Parra); and several chapbooks. She is the winner of several poetry prizes and was recently shortlisted for Montreal International Poetry Prize.